Script to Manifest

It's Time to Design & Attract Your Dream Life (Even if You Think it's Impossible Now)

Law of Attraction Short Reads, Book 7

By Elena G. Rivers

Copyright Elena G. Rivers © 2020

All rights reserved. No part of this publication may be reproduced, stored in a retrieval system, or transmitted, in any form or by any means, electronic, mechanical, photocopying, recording, or otherwise, without the author and the publishers' prior written permission.

The scanning, uploading, and distribution of this book via the Internet or any other means without the author's permission are illegal and punishable by law. Please purchase only authorized electronic editions and do not participate in or encourage electronic piracy of copyrighted materials.

Elena G. Rivers © Copyright 2020 - All rights reserved.

ISBN: 9798701965131

Legal Notice:

This book is copyright protected—it for personal use only.

Disclaimer Notice:

Please note the information contained in this book is for inspirational and entertainment purposes only. Every attempt has been made to provide accurate, up to date, and completely reliable information. No warranties of any kind are expressed or implied. Readers acknowledge that the author is not engaging in the rendering of legal, financial, health, medical, or professional advice. By reading this book, the reader agrees that under no circumstances are we responsible for any losses, direct or indirect, which are incurred as a result of the use of the information contained within this book, including, but not limited to, errors, omissions, or inaccuracies.

The information provided in this book is for entertainment purposes only. If you are struggling with serious problems, including chronic illness, mental instability, or legal issues, please consult with your local registered health care or legal professional as soon as possible. This book is not a substitute for professional or legal advice

Contents

Script to Manifest 1
Introduction 8
Script to Manifest Your Desires 8
Chapter 1 The Life-Changing Secrets of Scripting Revealed 20
Using Numbers to Manifest Faster 25
The 3x33 method and its variations for busy people 27
Do You Speak, Think, and Act to Manifest? Or Do You Block Your Manifestations Without Even Knowing? 29
How do you know how to make the right decision and script about the right things? 32
The Hidden Dangers of Not Letting Go 38
The Ivory Tower Scripting Trap to Avoid!. 42
Chapter 2 LOA for Skeptics (Why It Will Work for You If You Choose So!) 51
Chapter 3 Why You Can't Afford Not to Protect Your Dreams! 56
Chapter 4 The Secrets to True Empowerment with Scripting 60

Chapter 5 Your Questions Answered.......... 71

Chapter 6 Powerful Law of Attraction Meditation to Connect with Your Higher Self 87

Conclusion – Trust Yourself...................... 93

Introduction

Script to Manifest Your Desires

If you have a wish you'd like to manifest, you've come to the right place. This book will teach you everything you need to know about scripting so that you can start living your life by design.

But, before we dive into it, I want to be 100% honest and transparent with you. Even though scripting is one of my favorite Law of Attraction (LOA) methods, and I practice it every day, it will not work for everyone.

As someone who has been studying, researching, and teaching LOA for years and is particularly fond of the scripting method, I can tell you right here, right now, that it will not work for you in the following cases:

- Case 1 - Scripting will not work if the goal or wish you desire to manifest is not intrinsically yours, or you don't feel any connection with it. For example, you come across some random goal as you think it is expected of you, or because everyone around you is doing it. Perhaps everyone you know is manifesting amazing travels. And so, you think you should travel too because everyone is posting about their globe-trotting adventures on social media. But maybe you're not really into traveling, or you are, but you want to do things your way and visit different places. Whatever the goal is, make sure it's your own!

- Case 2 - The same is also true if you're chasing validation or significance. For example, you want to manifest a Ferrari or Lamborghini because you want other people to give you more respect and call you successful.

Let me explain. There's nothing wrong with desiring nice cars or other "toys" if you're genuinely passionate about them. But ask yourself this: are you a person who can handle and maintain expensive toys without getting freaked out?

Because when you manifest something, you receive the whole package, so you need to understand exactly what you're getting into.

In one of my other books, I shared the story of an acquaintance who manifested a big lottery win in her home country. Unfortunately, she lost it all because she had no idea how to handle large amounts of money; she even got in trouble with her local tax office. The reasons she originally wanted to manifest money were to feel loved and significant. She experienced those emotions fleetingly while having money, but then she lost it all and ended up exactly where she was before winning the lottery. Luckily, she used her experience as an essential life lesson and decided to do the inner work. As a result, she transformed her mindset and energy to become a person who can handle "the whole manifestation package." Now, she's manifesting abundance through her new business. She loves it! She no longer chases validation or approval; instead, she focuses on adding value to the world and providing an excellent service to her clients while manifesting her own money (and being very good at managing it!).

So, just a word of warning here! Are you ready to handle the whole package? Or do you want something purely because it will make you "look better"?

- Case 3 - You want to manifest something out of fear because you don't love yourself. An example of such a mindset is when a person "tries hard" to manifest love and romance, simply because they don't love themselves. They are desperate to find a partner: either to feel loved; or because they fear being single. Unfortunately, such a mindset can lead to negative manifestations. For example, a person can manifest a relationship that is draining or abusive for both parties. A much better and more empowering mindset is when a person already loves themselves and then intends to manifest a dream partner because they love the idea of sharing their life with someone else. They don't need another person to feel loved because they already feel whole and complete. Instead, they desire to manifest a partner from a place of love and with the intention of being in a healthy relationship. They are not desperate while trying to escape the feeling of being alone. So, ask yourself: do you want to manifest because you genuinely love your goals and desires, and you feel good about getting closer to them, or do you want to manifest to escape the pain and you are using your manifestations as a quick "cure"?

- Case 4 - Scripting might not be useful if you don't like writing things down. The scripting method is perfect for "journaling junkies" like me. We love making notes, and we adore having different journals. We actually look forward to our little rituals around writing, planning, expecting, and whatnot. It's fun! I don't know about you, but when I go to bed, I'm already excited for the next morning because I know that I'm going to be enjoying a pleasant morning cup of coffee while doing my little scripting ritual. It's fun for me, so I don't need to "try to stay motivated" or discipline myself to do it.

I always say – different strokes for different folks. You know who you are and what you naturally like or don't like. And since like attracts like and everything happens for a reason, I'm sure that most of the readers I attract are into the same or similar stuff that I'm into.

So, my guess is that you enjoy getting new journals and filling them with your desires.

But I also know that some of you might be getting this book out of curiosity. Or perhaps you are previewing a free sample before getting invested in it, which is a brilliant thing to do.

Once again, don't force yourself into a method just because everyone is doing it. If you're not into journaling, allow yourself to dive into other LOA ritual – have a look at my book catalog and pick something you feel naturally attracted to.

There is one little exception, though. You can learn more about scripting and apply its principles to mindfully formulate your wishes and re-program your subconscious mind while using a different vehicle. For example, a friend of mine learned the scripting method from me, but she's one of those people who don't really like writing things down in their journals. So, what she did instead was, she wrote her vision just once, and then she recorded it. She listens to it while commuting to work, which amounts to a solid hour a day. One of the things she put on her vision was:

"I'm so happy and grateful that my salary is always rising, and I always attract unexpected streams of income; because now I can take care of my family and live a life of fun!".

Within just a few weeks of doing her "audio scripting" while driving to work, she had already manifested a significant salary raise, and one of her side businesses also took off! Now, she's correspondingly manifesting a consistent monthly passive income from her ventures.

- Case 5 - And finally, the most important point I need to make is that scripting will not work if you just use it as a technique without fully understanding the central law of attraction and manifestation principle, which is:

It's not about what you do. It's about who you are and who you become.

And, *it's not about what you want. It's about who you are.*

You manifest what you hold inside.

In other words, it's all about your self-image. For example, you may "try hard" to make more money. You are looking for a new job, business opportunity, or some investments to become a six-figure earner. And yes, from a logical standpoint, it's a pretty smart thing to do. Unfortunately, if you don't already think and feel like a six-figure earner, chances are you will sabotage your efforts. I've seen it time and time again, and I've been there myself; I spent years chasing and chasing.

It was only when I decided to see myself as the person I wanted to become that I actually became that person, and things began to change. So, the first thing you need to do is to decide who you desire to become. Most people fail with manifesting their true desires because they mindlessly "try" to focus on what they want, without ever even attempting to change themselves. It's like trying to alter the reflection in the mirror without changing the person or object standing in front of it. I don't know about you, but I think it's total madness. Although, I don't want to get arrogant and judgmental because I've also been guilty of chasing my "wants" without wondering how to change myself.

As they say, the devil is in the details. It's sad but true. Many people think they already know "all this self-image stuff" because they know who they want to become in terms of status. But, they still do it wrong because they focus more on what they dislike about their old selves and they hardly ever think about their new, empowered selves. In alignment with such a negative mindset, they are still stuck in the past; blaming, judging, and criticizing. They never take any proactive action to upgrade who they are; their feelings, thoughts, behaviors, or skills.

I highly recommend you do this exercise right here and right now by answering the following questions in as much detail as you can (by the way, this is a fantastic pre-scripting preparation exercise!).

It's time to explore your New Self:

- How do you react when things don't go your way?
- Do you choose to complain and feel like a victim? Or do you choose to use unfavorable circumstances as valuable life lessons to help grow and improve yourself?
- How do you feel about learning and investing in yourself? What about the people you surround yourself with? Are they into reality creation?

Do they have goals, ambitions, and desires that they love working towards?
- How do you treat yourself, your body, and your mind?
- How do you talk to yourself?
- Do you choose to focus on your progress? Or are you still stuck in your old ways, feeling guilty about what went wrong?
- How much time do you need to let go?
5 minutes, 5 days, or 5 years?
- What movies do you play in your mind?
- Do you consciously use your mind to visualize what can go well?
Or do you choose to play negative movies in your mind?
- How do you fuel your body?
- Do you choose to eat healthy, whole, nutritionally balanced foods?
- How do you feel about investing in your health and wellbeing?
- What do you do when you feel stressed?
Do you choose to go for a walk, meditate, or watch an inspirational video?
Or are you stuck inside, feeling bad, scrolling through social media, and drinking or smoking?

We are doing this pre-scripting exercise for a reason. And, as you have probably noticed, for now, we don't focus on things such as what clothes you wear, where you live and what car you drive.

First things first! I see so many people discovering the concept of self-image and jumping into superficial self-image creation such as:

My new self wears designer clothes and lives in a nice neighborhood; my new self is a six-figure earner, and my new self attracts fantastic relationships.

And no, I'm not saying it's bad to want nice clothes and things, but once again, you are focusing on "what," not on "who". You believe you are working on your new self-image, whereas in reality, you still think like your old self, but with nice things around you.

In other words, you want to change the reflection in the mirror without wanting to change the person in front of it. It's all about your mindset, habits, reactions, behaviors, and energy. So before you get into scripting, design a new, powerful self-image with better habits, a more empowered mindset, and new behaviors. It's as simple as that.

Back to my story with scripting…

Yes, I used scripting as my primary manifestation method. However, I was already crystal clear on what made me tick, who I was, and what my authentic desires were. I got rid of all the "inner noise" and superficial goals.

Whatever it is that you do, remember you are sending out signals to the Universe all the time, even when you're not practicing any particular LOA technique or method such as scripting. So be sure to regularly check-in with your mindset and energy.

Let's go back to our previous example. Let's say you desire to manifest a six-figure job. So, how do you feel now when checking your bank account? Empowered? Or ashamed? How do you think and walk? Where do you go on vacations? What charities do you donate to?

A person could have the best scripting method ever and spend hours scripting every day. However, they could also go about their day and do their activities feeling hopeless, therefore negating any positive signals they sent out during their scripting sessions.

No wonder it doesn't work for some people. Or, we could say, it does work because the LOA always works.

However, it may not be working in their favor because their mindset and energy are still in a negative vibration.

What we want is full alignment!

You want to stay in check 24/7 and protect your mind and energy from negative influences as much as you can. Yes, use scripting as your secret method to remain focused on the positive. But also, strive to catch any negative habits or patterns you may be still holding onto and promise yourself to mindfully release them.

Don't feel bad about yourself when you experience a negative emotion. It's just a sign for you to let go. It's only feedback from the Universe reminding you to keep releasing your old vibrations while cleansing your mindset and energy.

Scripting will help you stay focused and grounded, and as you go through the techniques shared in this book, you will be raising your vibration. You will feel amazing. Your energy and mindset will shift, and every day, you will love yourself and your reality deeper and deeper, therefore attracting more good things, people, and circumstances into your life!

So now, with this pretty long intro out of the way, let's talk about scripting!

Chapter 1

The Life-Changing Secrets of Scripting Revealed

The main goal of scripting is to support your desire by giving it all your attention, energy, and focus. It makes you get used to your wishes so that they no longer feel far away. In other words, with scripting, you can fuse yourself with your vision instead of putting it on a pedestal. It's also very relaxing and creative because you get to empower yourself with some highly vibrational words.

Unfortunately, in this day and age, most people use a very disempowering language, which, more often than not, keeps them trapped in old, negative energies.

But with scripting, you can choose beautiful, confident, and vibrationally charged words to manifest your desires with joy and ease. Yes, it's all about writing to feel good! It's so much fun because you can formulate your wish list and become a mindful creator of your life.

The primary key to coming up with your wish list is that it must resonate with you. For example, let's say you write:

"I love how I feel knowing that I could easily manifest my dream partner."

Or:

"I love how I feel knowing that I could easily manifest a six-figure job."

"I love how I feel knowing that I could manifest my dream house."

What are the primary emotions you experience?

If you feel excited, expectant, happy, and positive, and you can see yourself as a person who's already living in your dream reality (even if you don't know the *how*), then your wish is truly yours.

The use of the phrase: *"I love how I feel knowing that I could easily manifest ...."* allows you to indicate your desire in a way that makes it real for you. When this happens, you send out a positive vibration to the Universe. In alignment with that, it doesn't matter how often you read or say your wish statement each day.

You want to focus on the quality of your vibration instead, and the best way to do this is to make sure you're working on your true goals, wishes, and desires. In other words, they must come from your heart and soul, and you must be able to see and feel yourself already living your dream!

Your main job is to identify what you want and give it positive attention, energy, and focus, knowing that you are sending out a positive vibration as you do.

Eliminate your doubts and negative vibrations by focusing on what can go well and why you deserve to manifest your desires.

Let's have a look at some examples to help you come up with your own ideas. Remember, it's not about copying other people's scripts word for word. Although yes, you could do that, if it feels right for you. However, you can also use them as inspiration to help you write your own.

Example Scripts:

Sample Script to Attract More Customers/Clients/Contracts:

- I am in the process of attracting and allowing everything I need to do, know and have to attract my ideal client/customer/contract.

This script uses the phrase "I'm in the process." This phrase is recommended for people who tend to give up on their goals because they feel overwhelmed and think their destination is too far away. So, if you create a statement such as, "*I now make 20k a month every month,*" and it feels like a big stretch for you, so because of that, you start doubting yourself, you can soften it up by using the phrase "*I'm in the process.*" For example: "*I'm now in the process of raising my income to 20k a month, and I love the person I'm becoming. It's so empowering*".

More examples:

- I love how it feels when I attract high-end clients. All my clients are educated, love to invest in themselves, are polite, do the work and pay on time. I love it when they recommend my services to their friends, because like attracts like.

- I love the idea of receiving emails or phone calls from my ideal clients, especially when they get great results and want to share them with me. I love how it feels to

know that my ideal clients are so impressed with their results that they tell others about my services, thus attracting more ideal clients. I love the idea of working 8-10 hours a week as a coach to my ideal clients. The Law of Attraction is in the process of developing and orchestrating this now. I just love it because it feels so magical!

Example script to attract more abundance:

- I am in the process of attracting and allowing everything I need to attract my abundance. I love how it feels when I am gifted free lunch, coffee, or dinner. It always works! I am excited whenever I get free advice, free drinks, free parking, a coupon, a discount, or someone offers to help me for free. I love the idea of getting money from unknown sources. The Law of Attraction is in the process of developing and orchestrating this now. It really feels magical!

Example script to attract more love:

- I am in the process of attracting and allowing everything I need to attract my ideal love relationship.

- I love the idea of going on walks with my dream partner. I love the idea of packing a lunch and eating at the beach with my love. I love how it feels to know that

the conversation is positive, uplifting, and supportive. The Universal Law of Attraction is in the process of developing and orchestrating this now. It feels so magical!

Using Numbers to Manifest Faster

As Pythagoras once said: *"Numbers rule the world."*

And, we can use this to our advantage by leveraging the 3x33 method.

3x33 manifestation is a powerful Law of Attraction writing technique that combines the power of spiritual numbers, intention, focus, emotion, and repetition to fill the subconscious mind with the desire or goal we wish to manifest.

But before I dive into the method itself, I'd like to explain why it works. When you work with the 3x33 method, you activate the energy of number 3; the Divine feminine on the Kabbalistic tree of life. Feminine energy is the energy of life and creation.

So, if you have a series of situations and projects that are scattered or remain unfinished, it's time to use the Divine feminine energy with your scripting rituals. It's all about writing your intentions from a place of love and in a transparent way.

The 3x33 method and its variations for busy people

You first choose an intention (something you want to manifest), and then you create a simple statement about that intention.

Then you write out this affirmation 33 times a day for 3 days.

I know, I know. You're probably thinking, "What? 33 times? That's too many!"

And here is where I need to clarify one thing... It's all about quality over quantity... Although yes, the original method indeed tells us that we should write 33 affirmations every day for 3 days, the most important thing is your pure intention.

It's all about being in the present moment while writing your affirmations. You want to think and feel how blessed you are to be receiving. This is why it's absolutely fine to make modifications, such as write your affirmation 3 times for the next 33 days (my favorite idea because it helps you develop mindful consistency and discipline without burning yourself out).

Whatever you choose to do, it's all about mindful repetition; write 33 times for 3 days, 3 times for 33 days, or 9 times for 3 days. Our beliefs are formed in our minds through continuous repetition of that thought over and over again.

Don't forget to use "I am" at the beginning of your affirmations. Since our mind is already accustomed to being addressed with "I am" we will continue this "I am" pattern of internal dialogue in our affirmations as well.

Your affirmations can also include words that express positive emotions such as *happy, grateful, feeling blessed, lucky, etc.*

These are powerful words because they naturally put you in a state of bliss, gratitude, and abundance. Therefore, use them lavishly in your scripted affirmations.

As you probably already know, your affirmations, statements, or scripts (whatever you want to call them) must be written in the present tense. Use a sentence that begins with "I am now...", "I have now...", etc. The idea is to feel grateful; like your wish has already been fulfilled.

Also, don't use the phrase "I want" in your affirmations. By saying, "I want," you automatically imply that you don't have it, therefore sending out a very negative vibration to the Universe. Some unhappy souls get stuck in "wanting" for years, and it only helps them manifest how to be a better "wannabe."

Do You Speak, Think, and Act to Manifest? Or Do You Block Your Manifestations Without Even Knowing?

Your language patterns are fundamental, and there are many words I highly recommend you choose to let go of accordingly.

For example, instead of saying:

"I am trying to,"

say:

"I am playing," or "I am experimenting."

To say that you are trying automatically allows the massive possibility of failure and even a lack of genuine commitment. For example, instead of saying, "I am trying this new business idea," I prefer to say: "I am experimenting with this new opportunity," or "I am learning about it."

You see, when you experiment or learn, there's no space to fail.

When you experiment, you always get a result that will teach you something. There's no such thing as a negative outcome; it's just an outcome, which is some kind of valuable feedback and data.

Instead of saying "I want to," say "I choose to," or "I intend to". Both are much more powerful!

Wanting makes us wannabes. By definition, a wannabe wants something because he or she doesn't have it. If you're a pro at something, you already have it and you do it. It's absolutely normal for you.

As we have already mentioned, you can also say that you're in the process of manifesting something. Expressing that you are "in the process" is an excellent way to help you reduce resistance. This is extremely helpful if you set big goals and massive intentions, and maybe you get a bit nervous. If you state that you're in the process, it'll calm you down; almost on autopilot.

Move on with clarity and be decisive. For example, if you desire to become a business person, focus on one venture until successful. You can't be halfway in and halfway out.

Also, avoid "maybes" and "when I get this, then I'll..." thought patterns. Why not get there directly?

Maybe there's a direct flight.

Alignment is vital since you don't want to be in chaos vibrations or don't want to manifest "maybes" or "I'll do this when..." situations.

How do you know how to make the right decision and script about the right things?

Well, I can't tell you precisely, as I can't make any decisions for you. You see, I used to let other people decide for me, and then whenever I manifested what I didn't want, I'd blame them and not myself. I want to stay away from such energy. Making decisions is also a muscle. Follow your gut!

Be specific, and don't be vague. This is where scripting can help. You can use your script as a tool to help you "taste your new reality;" to see what you like and how you feel. You can also script to stretch your mindset and realize where your weak points are to let them go.

Reverse engineer what worked for you. Think about all the fantastic things you've achieved so far. I'm sure you were specific, that idea just came to your mind, and you knew it was the right thing to do. Reverse engineering what already worked for you is one of the best tools because you and your own life are your best mentors, seriously!

Please note, journaling and scripting can't be done from a place of scarcity. It's not about how much time you spend writing in your journal or what kind of journal you use, just like it's not about how many vision boards you make and how long you visualize for. It's all about your feelings and the emotion behind them. Yes, sometimes you may find yourself feeling like a robot, so be aware of it and focus on something that makes you feel good. Dance, or do some quick yoga pose.

You attract who you are, so if you feel empty, then you'll attract like. Keep your mind and soul open to different sensations.

Some people prefer to record themselves and then listen to their intentions. Audio scripting works for many of my friends, but I prefer traditional scripting and journaling.

Whenever scripting, what I highly recommend is to first be in high vibration or to meditate beforehand.

After you do that, get clear on what you intend to manifest. Then, you can visualize, write, or affirm. Whatever you choose to do, make sure to include lots of positive, expressive words: words that make you feel good and give you an emotional high. Deeply feel the emotions while doing so. Finally, just let it go and move on with your daily activities with good energy.

Using different manifestation methods such as scripting isn't meant to obtain something for you. Manifestation methods are used to tune your vibration to become a vibrational match to your desire.

If you're practicing scripting every day because you're feeling anxious or impatient about your desire, then you'll massively put off your success. So, use scripting to feel good about your desire. I always say it's not so much about what you do, but how you do it.

When I do my gratitude journaling or scripting, I do it because it feels good to me, and I enjoy living in the moment of mindfully putting my desires on paper. Then, I know I'm on a vibrational match to them.

The question I very often get asked is:

So, do I just write about the experiences that I want to have? Because I don't really want anything materialistic. I want to manifest health and happiness. How do I do it the right way?

Answer:

There's really no "wrong" way to journal anything; it's different for everyone. Just make sure you're writing in the present tense - as if you're currently living the life you want and feel the emotions while you do it. Be specific about the happy moments you intend to manifest. For example, "Every weekend, I enjoy amazing parties in beautiful locations. I eat sophisticated dinners with interesting people. I laugh and have fun."

Or: "Every evening, I hang out with my kids, and we laugh and play."

Manifesting isn't just about money. Even if a person wants to manifest financial abundance, the subconscious mind finds it hard to understand the money and numbers; however, it can easily align with the feeling of freedom and happiness.

At the same time, many of my readers who tried to manifest abundance for years (yeah, they tried, and nothing happened) suddenly began manifesting unexpected income just by focusing on manifesting happiness first.

Some food for thought!

I can personally attest to the holistic effectiveness of focusing on manifesting happiness and peace of mind. The rest becomes easier, and all the resistance gets removed.

Be very mindful of your language. Use words that empower and send out the vibration of conviction and confidence, not lack or unworthiness.

The affirmation should convey that the desire is here and is already part of our reality.

Also, remember to have fun with your desires, but don't get too obsessed. Ask yourself, if you already had your desires, how would you feel about them? Would you feel stressed that it's "taking too long"? Of course not. Because it would feel normal to you.

This is where the Normalization Method comes in. It's as simple as affirming: *It's normal for me to...*

Example: *It's normal for me to attract high-quality clients.*

It's normal for me to travel the world while doing what I love for a living.

It's normal for me to work my dream job!

It's normal for me to feel amazing in my body.

It's normal for me to have a six-figure business.

It's normal for me to feel healthy and energized. In fact, every day, I feel better and better. I thrive.

It's normal for me to enjoy vibrant health!

It's normal for me to attract kind and loving people into my life.

The Hidden Dangers of Not Letting Go

You also need to master the art of letting go. Once again, no complicated rituals are required. For our scripting purposes, letting go means mindfully addressing any doubts, worries, or anxiety associated with our intention.

For example, let's say you keep writing, "I'm so grateful I'm now making a steady six-figures in my job/business. I love the people I work with; it's so much fun!".

And then you suddenly start experiencing a negative emotion, thinking:

"OMG, but what if I make more money and I begin to lose my friends? What if they start feeling jealous or feel bad?"

Many LOA teachers would tell you to dismiss it as some negative thought and just keep writing or reciting: *"Oh, but I'm a six-figure earner, and I'm so happy"* (but this can inadvertently create resistance and, more often than not, leads to you manifesting what you don't want, or sabotaging your efforts). However, we want to use any negative thoughts that come up as clues and valuable feedback.

So, take a break from writing or affirming, and ask yourself:

- *How would the new 2.0 version of myself think? Would I really feel that way?*

As a result, you may start coming up with different answers, therefore reducing resistance:

- *Well, I will find out who my real friends are. My real friends will be inspired, not jealous! And if they are motivated, then they too can reach more success if they want to.*

- *Life is not only about money. If some of my old friends are not into increasing their salaries and incomes, that's fine. We can still enjoy each other's company and talk about other passions and interests that we share.*

- *If I make more money, then I will be able to help those around me. I can already feel this great peace of mind that money can offer. I'm a good person, and money will amplify it. I can only feel good about myself because I'm an ambitious person, and I deserve a well-paying job or business.*

Or perhaps as you go writing your vision, you start worrying:

- Hmm...but if I make more money, my taxes will be more complicated. Is it really worth it?

And then, once again, explore that inner resistance. How would your 2.0 version think? Would they worry about it? Of course not. So, you can start soothing your subconscious mind by affirming:

- I can trust myself with making more money and doing my taxes. I always attract great people into my life. Now, I'm in the process of attracting a tax expert who can help me. It is a win-win! It's safe for me to make more money.

Maybe you will even feel inspired to book a consultation with a financial planner or a tax expert, acting exactly as if you were already making your desired income. If not, why not?

I used this exact same method to manifest my ideal weight without any restrictive dieting, just eating a whole food diet, most of the time. I remember writing down my affirmations while experiencing an incredible resistance, such as:

Oh, but if I lose weight, then my sister and family members will feel jealous. I mean, she used to be a ballet queen as a teen, and now she's put on weight. If I lose weight, she will feel bad, and so will my mom.

So, I began to explore that thought because I wanted to empower it and turn it into something positive. I visualized myself at my ideal weight. I saw my family telling me how great I looked and that they too feel inspired to lose weight, asking if I wanted to help them.

I began writing down a new affirmation:

I am so grateful for my ideal weight, healthy lifestyle, and incredible energy levels. I'm even more thankful that my loved ones could join me on this journey and reach their health and weight loss goals with me. Now, we go hiking together. We go to healthy organic restaurants together. We mindfully change our habits together, and it's so much fun!

It worked very well for all of us! Which proves the importance of exploring our negative thoughts and resistance. No, we don't dwell on the negative. We use it to transform our lives and manifest our dream reality with joy and ease, for the highest good of all involved.

Also, please note that some people are just not ready to change. Yes, they may judge you; they may criticize you because you decided to shine and live life on your own terms. But don't allow their negative vibration to destroy your dreams. Don't be a people pleaser. Choose to raise up and live to your new standards. Those who get inspired will reach out for help, and those who get jealous only harm themselves, not you.

So, never feel inadequate for formulating new desires and affirmations aligned with your unique vision for life. Stop asking for approval and concerning yourself with what other people think of you.

Focus on the fact that there are numerous techniques to reinforce the reality you long for. One of the most powerful is the written word, and you are already using it to mindfully create your own reality!

The Ivory Tower Scripting Trap to Avoid!

Sometimes you may find yourself creating an affirmation that eventually stops being fun or loses its meaning. It no longer feels right for you because your goals have shifted. Then, you may find yourself feeling stuck.

Remember, this is just feedback. Any negativity you experience in your mind can be transformed into a new, positive vision. You can always change direction!

To do this, you must create a vision for your desired life that is as detailed as possible. Write about it in your journal. Design your perfect life, your expected life. Besides writing about it, allow yourself to live it as much as you can, right here and right now.

I keep a daily diary of my desired life. I use it to capture a life in which I already have everything I want, and consequently, the Universe does not hesitate to follow my clear instructions.

Below are the three journaling tips you absolutely can't miss:

1.- Be super detailed and follow your intuition

For example, if you want to attract a perfect house, you can write:

"I am grateful to wake up every day in my wide and comfortable bed from which I can see the sea and the sky through the terrace window. The sheets are blue, soft, and smooth. I can hear the seagulls and the sound of the waves breaking in the distance. I love the smell of

the sea. I drink coconut latte on my terrace while planning my day. My partner calls me for breakfast. We're going to enjoy some delicious homemade pancakes and marmalade."

When writing, use all your senses: see, hear, touch, smell and taste your new reality.

By writing things down in detail, you will also find it much easier to visualize your desires.

The first step is always to capture what you want, not what you don't want. Always write in the present and in the first person. Mentally screenshot the best and most exciting parts of your dream so that you can later use them in your visualizations. This can be a terrific complementary method.

Many people fail with this exercise because they write in the future tense while just "hoping" for something to manifest. And tomorrow never comes. Instead, you want to write with conviction and unleash the power of the present moment.

Remember, the Universe doesn't like to feel confused. So, express yourself clearly, say what you want, and supercharge it by feeling good. You deserve it, and you have it.

Accompany your writing with photos and drawings that reinforce your vision. For example, you can use pictures of a beach sunrise, an elegant bedroom, and a superior interior design.

Use your favorite colors to highlight the most relevant words you write. Colors can elevate your vision and make it vibrate at a higher level.

2.- Your scripting ritual should be a blessing, not an obligation.

This is very important. Never write out of obligation, do it only if you want to. Also, don't think that by writing more, you will attract your dreams faster.

In nature, everything needs time. For example, it takes nine months to give birth to a baby. It's not that with nine women, it will take only a month.

The most important thing is the vibration you emit when you write. You are really living what you describe in your journal.

If one day you don't feel like writing or can't focus on it for whatever reason, that's fine. You can re-read what you have already written or simply rest... Tomorrow is another day, and you will feel refreshed. This is not a competition, and you have nothing to prove. Enjoy writing or don't write!

If you don't have time for writing, ask yourself, *What can I do to read or feel my vision every day?*

- Perhaps I can take a picture of my writings and keep it on my phone. Whenever I feel tempted to mindlessly scroll on social media, I can scroll on my vision instead.

- Perhaps I can record my vision and listen to it in my car on my commute to work.

There's always a plan B. There's still something to fall back on!

3.- Support your writing with action.

Do whatever you can do to keep moving forward. Take inspired action. Start acting "as if." If you're in the process of manifesting a significant salary raise, talk to a financial planner or accountant who has experience working with wealthy people.

If you are in the process of manifesting a healthy body, start going to healthy food stores, or book a holistic cooking class. Invest in a professional consultation with a naturopath or nutritionist. Instead of watching TV, go for a walk.

If you desire to be well-known for your work; you want to be the number-one-to-go-to expert, perhaps your next bold step would involve enrolling in some professional course. Or maybe you could talk to a marketing expert to learn how to put yourself out there, get leverage and get your work known by more people.

If you are an entrepreneur who is now scaling your business, well, perhaps the next step will be to change your business structure. Maybe you are too big now to do your business as a sole proprietor. Perhaps it's time to upgrade and register as a company or a corporation. How about hiring employees? The next step would be to talk to an expert and get familiar with a new plan.

Yes, it will feel very uncomfortable at first. Your mind will tell you, *"Oh, but I'm not there yet. I can't do this. Maybe, I need to wait."*

But guess what, it's all about Calculated Vibration Raises! Yes, you also need to stretch yourself and show the Universe that you are committed. You already are the person who can handle the Whole Manifestation Package. You can handle growth; you can handle talking to financial experts; you can handle eating a healthy diet; you can handle joining the gym. You can handle whatever it is that the new, 2.0 version of you is already doing with your eyes closed, pretty much automatically.

So, if it's a house you want, you can visit it. Arrange a visit with a real estate agent. Enjoy the process of touring your dream house and feel the energy; imagine yourself living in it. Now it will be much easier for you to write about it. You can even declare, "This is my house."

You can't fail: you either succeed, or you learn. You can only get closer to your goals.

It's like a little kid who gets new shoes that turn out to be a bit too big. Eventually, he or she will grow into them. So, don't be afraid. Your time will come!

The best part is that you will be someone who can handle them when you manifest your desires. You will not sabotage your success by reverting back to your old self, old feelings, thoughts, and actions that no longer resonate with your new goals.

Unfortunately, most people miss that part. They want to write about their desires, but they never take any aligned action. Sometimes, they may manifest what they want, but since they are not used to the Full Manifestation Package, they can't handle their achievements. For example, a person can manifest a rise in their income.

But, because they never prepared for it and never talked to a professional financial planner or high-level accountant, they may mismanage their money.

Don't be that person; be a smart manifestor. Prepare yourself, do your research, talk to experts. Learn and grow. Leave your comfort zone.

Remember, if the goals you desire to manifest are indeed yours, it means that your 2.0 version already knows how to handle the Full Manifestation Package. You want to fuse yourself with your new version by gradually changing your feelings, thoughts, actions, and habits.

Things that used to irritate you don't bother you anymore. Your old problems no longer exist. If anything, you get new "problems," which are better quality problems.

Example – Old self: *It's hard to pay the bills!*

New Self: *Money is no longer a problem. In fact, I can start investing. My new quality "problem" is that I need to find a good investment expert to learn from.*

You want a new car? Visit the dealership. If it's a new job, try visiting their offices. Talk to people who work there. Maybe there is a way to do business with them now?

Seeing your desire in reality will motivate you and help you to persevere.

Today is the perfect day to start with this diary of your desired life. What do you want? What is your dream? Capture it with your mindful scripting rituals.

Remember that the Universe will always give you what you feel you deserve. Feel good, and you will attract good.

Chapter 2

LOA for Skeptics (Why It Will Work for You If You Choose So!)

Have you ever wondered why, after hearing about a specific book, concept, word, term, or number, you suddenly start seeing it everywhere? Perhaps you've joined some spiritual communities where everyone is talking about seeing repetitive numbers such as 11:11 or 22:22. And now, you too can see repetitive numbers all around you, and become to feel intrigued! Is it magic? Or something else? Personally, I think it's magic because we are magical, and so are our brains! But there's also a scientific explanation behind it.

You see what you choose to focus on. You see repetitive numbers because of the big bundle of nerves sitting at the end of your brainstem: the Reticular Activating System (RAS).

The RAS is what makes the Law of Attraction work. And it always works. It's totally up to you to choose to wake up and begin to consciously program yourself, scripting your life in the way you desire.

Your RAS registers what you focus on and creates filters to display what's on your mind. In other words, it uses its smart algorithms to show you precisely what it thinks you most desire to see.

There is a little problem though! While the RAS is good at showing you what it thinks you want to see or what drives your attention, it isn't great at understanding what you truly want.

It can only determine what you focus on - that's it. So ask yourself, what's on your mind? What do you feed it with? Do you focus on what you desire?

For example, if your desire is to buy a beautiful home, but you keep focusing on how impossible it is to get a mortgage and that everything is so expensive while salaries are going down, well, guess what your RAS is going to do?

It will quickly figure out, "OK, you are looking for more proof and evidence to see how impossible or even dangerous it is to buy your own house. Let's do this. Your wish is my command!"

Simultaneously focus on what you want by using scripting, good feelings, and visualizations. Your RAS will do everything it can to make you more aware of fantastic house opportunities waiting for you.

The amount of effort it takes is pretty much the same once you understand the importance of positive focus.

Although yes, to be absolutely honest with you, it may feel a bit draining when you first get started. It's like going to a Spirituality Gym and building up your Positive Focus Muscle while making RAS work in alignment with your desires.

So, what do you choose?

Choosing to ignore your RAS is especially dangerous in today's social media world, where it's easy to fall into false information that reinforces what you already believe, not necessarily what's right or in alignment with what you want.

This is the reason why I deleted most of my social media profiles and stopped scrolling. Instead, I concentrated on doing inner work while mindfully working on my focus. As a result of my work, my RAS began presenting me with positive filters that would lead me to my goals.

This is the real science behind the Law of Attraction. What you focus on expands, and it eventually becomes your reality. It happens pretty much on autopilot, and yet most people never wake up. They never even attempt to re-program their inner filters while changing their existence. It's a question of choice.

So, why do I mention all this? Well, perhaps as you're reading this book, you're starting to feel doubtful and thinking, *will this work for me?*
But whether you choose positivity or negativity, the fact remains: What you think about, you bring about.

To mindfully create your dream reality, the first step is to see it in your current one.

When you look at the world through a positive, creative lens, opportunities to attract more positivity just pop-up, and it feels like magic!

You can train your RAS and use it to deliver inspiration and the next steps to follow right to your doorstep. Also, remember, positivity isn't just about smiling or pretending to be positive so that everyone around you says: "Oh wow, you are so spiritual and positive."

Real positivity is about being able to step up and solve problems in a creative and empowering way. Genuine positivity is when you are resilient and know how to persevere. So, choose to see the light because there is always light at the end of the tunnel. You are that light!

Chapter 3

Why You Can't Afford Not to Protect Your Dreams!

When you decide to shine your light while emitting more and more positive energy, creating personal and professional success, some negative individuals may attempt to belittle you or make you believe that it's not safe for you to grow.

Remember to stay focused on your journey, no matter what. Different people make different choices, and some people just choose to stay where they are.

Be very mindful of:

- who you surround yourself with

- what you share and with who

- your authentic desires - after all, you want to focus on what you want!

The best way to "deal with negativity" is to allow yourself to get out of it by focusing on positive thoughts, actions, and feelings.

For example, as I began to grow as an author, I quickly noticed that some people who I thought were my "friends" began to gossip or even make jokes about it. I had two choices: go back to where I was before: negative, sad, broke, and taking part in their "drama," or keep raising my vibration; learning, growing, investing in myself, and allowing new people into my life.

I don't know about you, but I have already wasted lots of time in my life, just trying to please others or make them like me.

I would even say I was addicted to "what they will think of me?" at some stage. Well, I had to let it go. I had to carry on doing the inner work while becoming a new person. Now, I'm no longer attracted to drama, gossip, or negativity. I refuse to take any part in it. No, thank you very much.

And this is the best tip I could ever give you: fill your day with as many positive activities as you can and make your inner work a priority. Accept that, as you continue on your Law of Attraction and scripting journey, you will be outgrowing some friends. But, here's one awesome thing to understand; at the same time, you will also be growing into new people, circumstances, and possibilities!

There is an exercise that I learned from Neuro-Linguistic Programing (NLP), and it's very effective in minimizing the effect that the influence of negative people can have on you - primarily, when it affects you explicitly. This exercise consists of redefining the frame of reference with which you see a negative person. You can do it in several ways, and it's lots of fun!

You can visualize that person with a clown nose. This way, every time they say something rude to you, imagine them with a giant clown nose and clown shoes. You can even paint their face if you want to. What they say now comes out of a clown's mouth, so there's no way it can adversely affect you!

You can also imagine that this negative person speaks to you from a tiny box, so you can hardly hear their words. You cannot understand what they say very well because they are in the box! They are so small, and their voice is so low. Therefore, what they say simply doesn't affect you.

You can design any other exercise of this kind that serves to redefine the frame. You are the one who dominates, and you are in an advantageous situation. By doing this, you put yourself in a position of strength that allows you to emit very high and positive vibrations. You create a kind of magnetic field around you, a powerful one that prevents the passage of bad energies while raising your self-esteem.

Remember, don't let other people divert you from your path. You are now scripting your dream reality, and it's in the process of manifesting. This is why protecting yourself and your energy is so important!

Now you understand the primary and most potent principles of scripting. You also know why your focus is essential and how to protect it from negative people and circumstances.

The following pages will give you more inspiration and empowerment to help you mindfully design your life with scripting.

Chapter 4

The Secrets to True Empowerment with Scripting

It's all about creating your own way of scripting. Use the fundamental principles outlined in this book as a template to start working with the Universal Laws. But also be mindful of doing things your way, and feel good about it!

Keep in mind that you need to allow yourself to have a whole life of success. There's no reason to limit yourself. You are not writing a to-do list while desperately trying to think: *"Oh, but will I have time for this today?"*

Instead, you are writing a book of your life, a life well-lived, a life you can be proud of. One of the best ways to do this is to write your scripts as if they were gratitude letters. This technique will help you align with total solutions and endless positive possibilities to help you design a wonderful life.

For example, I used to worry about finances. It was several years ago when I was in debt. Back then, I didn't know much about scripting.

Out of nowhere, I got inspired to write a gratitude letter to the Universe because I wanted to feel better about my situation. I already knew good feelings could help me manifest better things, and writing a gratitude letter seemed like an excellent idea.

So, I took a piece of paper (I wasn't a journaling junkie back then), and I wrote:

It feels so good to have all the money I need to pay my bills, live an extraordinary life, and save up. I'm glad that I finally found a way to get out of debt forever, and now, when I think about it, it seems like some past life.

Money flows abundantly. I don't need to worry about it. All I focus on is doing my passion for a living and helping other people.

I love what I do, and what I do loves me. I get rewarded for my work. Also, I love that I now finally have more time for self-care and can indulge in long walks on the beach. I live on a small island, where it's so peaceful and quiet; people are nice and friendly. I love this place.

Right now, as I'm writing this, I'm chilling on the beach, writing my gratitude letter thinking how far I've come. Thank You, Universe, for allowing me to live my best life.

After finishing my gratitude letter, I saved it in an old cookbook. A few years later, I found it as I was moving houses. And do you know the best part? Not only was I moving houses, but I was also re-locating to a small island in the Atlantic (Fuerteventura, Canary Islands), and it was exactly what I had written down in my gratitude letter.

Back then, I had no idea how it would happen. The vision literally came out of my subconscious mind as I allowed myself to be in a relaxed, positive state while letting in new energies and infinite possibilities. My vision made complete sense to me. I simply affirmed what I desired and sent out a clear signal to the Universe.

People always ask me what kind of goal to keep in mind while scripting. For example, *should you start small, just to test it and see if it works?*

My answer is, it depends on your mindset and energy.

After years of practicing the LOA, I realized that, for me, setting big goals works amazingly well because they open my mind up to new possibilities. But you must believe it's right for you and the goal must genuinely be yours. Otherwise, you will give up on it, saying, *oh, it's taking too long, it's not working.*

At the same time, many people start off with small goals because they feel insecure about themselves. And it's because of that negative energy that they don't manifest even a tiny dream. They are still thinking: *I guess I should keep shrinking my dreams, and maybe that way I can manifest something.*

So, first things first - get your mindset right, realize who you are and what you truly desire. Then, get your energy right and ask yourself: A*m I attempting to manifest from the energy of lack or abundance? Do I believe in myself? Do I realize that the creative power of the Universe is there to help me?*

Both small and high goal setting can be done successfully if you spend some time adjusting your mindset and energy by answering the above questions.

You can also do both. Set a big goal and treat it as your vision. Then, think of a small goal that serves as a milestone leading you to the bigger one (this is my favorite way of doing things). As you manifest your desires, don't forget to keep expressing your gratitude for all the milestones you've already reached and everything you learned on your journey.

Such an attitude will automatically help you get rid of guilt, shame, or hopelessness that you may experience if you focus too much on your mistakes.

For example, a professional woman is feeling stuck in her job. Her big goal is to be working for herself as a coach in her chosen field, making 10k a month.

Right now, it all seems so far away because in her current job, she's making 5k a month, and she doesn't even like what she does.

But, she still writes a gratitude letter to the Universe. She focuses on every detail in her vision:

Wow, I can't believe it. Today I finally gave my notice and will be leaving my job soon. What used to be my dream and my little side hustle is now making me 10k a month, and I love the work I do. I attract amazing clients who are ready to transform. They follow my programs and get fantastic results. Every day, I get an email or a message from a happy client telling me they recommended my work to their family and friends. The clients just keep coming, and they are all high-end clients. *The best part? I work much less than in my current job. In fact, I work only 4-5 hours a day, four days a week. I finally have more time for self-care and self-development, which allows me to develop innovative solutions and better programs for my clients. I'm getting better and better at marketing too! In fact, other coaches are reaching out to me, offering me money to help them market their services. I've never experienced so much abundance in my life! Thank You, Thank You, Thank You!*

After specifying her vision and getting very excited about it while already feeling grateful for it, she sets her first milestone: *I'm now making 1k a month or more from my side business as a coach.*

She aligns her actions, thoughts, and feelings with this milestone. She decides to *be* that milestone and truly live it. After all, it doesn't seem like something difficult; she can do it. So, she takes aligned and inspired action from a place of curiosity: *I wonder how it would feel to have that extra 1k a month in my pocket? What would I do with that money? I could easily save to go on a nice vacation, or I could begin to invest in myself and my coaching education. Or I could buy a nice camera and some equipment to start doing YouTube videos and attracting my dream clients.*

Even though she still doesn't have a nice camera or lightning, she already feels unstoppable. She swaps excuses for mindful action. She takes her smartphone and makes inspirational videos to upload to YouTube. In fact, every morning, while driving to work, she records an uplifting video, sharing her knowledge. At the end of each video, she offers personalized, 1:1 help. She's honest, open, and transparent; not afraid to share her personal struggles from a place of authenticity.

After a few weeks, she can easily manifest an extra 1k a month while still working in her job.

Wow, this is working! So, now let's start a new milestone. What about 3k a month?

Instead of looking for excuses, she looks for the evidence that it's already working for her and she can do it. She keeps stretching herself and her vibration in alignment with her new goals. She sees obstacles and challenges as lessons to learn and grow from.

Eventually, her vision becomes her reality, and she manifests a successful, 6-figure career doing what she loves for a living. Nothing can beat scripting, supercharged with the power of goal setting.

Please remember that you can use this methodology to improve all areas of your life! But, since most people that reach out to me desire to manifest more money, many of the examples of this book focus on money and numbers. Numbers don't lie – they can only tell us if we reach our goals or not. Remember, though, you can use scripting magnified with goal setting to enrich all areas of your life. This brings us to the next question.

People always ask me if it's possible to manifest multiple things at once. My answer is, it's up to you. If you think it's possible for you and you fully believe it, go for it.

Personally, I like to focus on one or two areas of my life at a time. It's because I understand that when you address the areas of life that need most of your attention, other things you desire may manifest automatically. I'm also a big believer in the power of focus.

When I first got started on my scripting journey, my main focus was on my writing and health. And as I began taking mindful action, transforming and manifesting my desires, other areas of my life such as relationships, finance, travel, and spirituality changed as well.

So, ask yourself, which area of your life requires most of your attention now? And which one is next?

For example, if you struggle with low energy and can't lose weight, perhaps you could start with your health. Write out your vision in detail and set your first milestone. Rinse and repeat. Remember to keep taking aligned action and start acting "as if." Allow yourself to move your body; go for lovely, rejuvenating walks instead of watching TV; and swap candy bars for fresh smoothies.

Book a consultation with a nutritionist or naturopath. Yes, the Universe will help by arranging many things for you, but you must keep taking aligned action, showing your commitment, and fusing yourself with your vision by gradually becoming a person who lives that vision. Treat your body like a temple, and other areas of your life will improve as well.

It's all about tapping into the thought process and vibration of what you desire and acting precisely as the 2.0 version of you would!

To sum up:

Step #1 - Start off by writing a letter to the Universe (or whomever you choose to see and identify as the source.

You can even write a letter to your higher self, God, your angels; it's really up to you). Be and feel thankful in advance for all your desires coming true.

Step #2 - Fuse yourself with your vision every day. You can read your letter or start writing about different elements of it in your journal. You can also record it and listen to it in your car. If you are really busy, you could even mentally screenshot your gratitude letter and carry it in your mind and heart.

The method I'm using now is that I combine this with my daily gratitude. Every day, I write down several things I'm grateful for, and then I intuitively start adding some elements from my vision, as if they already happened. It makes it so real for my inner mind! Also, I get excited writing about things I'm grateful for (already manifested in my reality), which makes me very confident in my manifestation powers. Then, I add something from my vision and can't help but feel gratitude for it.

Step #3 - If you are still looking for the "right way" to do this, remember that you are the right way. Just focus on really feeling your desires, and evoke emotion.

Step #4 Don't get too obsessed with your vision, torturing yourself with thoughts such as, "*Oh, when will it happen?*".

Just move on with your life and do your daily activities with joy. Know that something in you has already changed, and your external reality is changing too. Train your mind to start looking for positive proof and evidence of everything working out for you.

Step #5 - For some people, scripting can become robotic. If it does, take a break. Don't force it. The most important thing is to feel the emotion of your desire.

Step #6 - Enjoy it, and Happy Manifesting!

Chapter 5

Your Questions Answered

This chapter is designed to take your scripting journey to the next level by answering the most common questions that people have.

It will help you stay motivated and inspired to manifest faster!

Question: Does it matter what you write your vision on? Do I need a special journal or paper?

Answer: No. The Universe doesn't think, "you wrote in red ink, and on blue paper, so I'm not listening to you." Instead, it responds to how you feel about what you do. So, choose whatever works for you. If you get excited about your new journal and its beautiful paper, go for it.

If you like your old notebook, use it. And choose whatever color you want. Personally, I love red ink because it makes me feel in control. It makes me feel like the master of my own reality: someone who gets to correct what is out of alignment!

Question: Which one is better? Basic scripts or abundant stories?

Answer: I would suggest abundant stories with as much detail as possible. However, if you're feeling resistance, or can't come up with too much detail, don't worry for now. Start off with a basic script (it can even be one sentence) and go from there. As you begin to re-write your brain and focus on what you actually want while believing that you too can manifest your wildest dreams, your basic scripts will turn into great stories filled with positive emotions, and your reality will start to reflect this. Again, don't force it; let it come.

But also, be persistent and don't give up. Some people find it hard to come up with their vision. There's nothing to worry about, though. Keep exploring different scenarios and possibilities in your mind and start writing them down. This can be a tremendous pre-scripting exercise. When you're ready, come up with your real, authentic vision!

Sometimes you feel like you want so many things but are not too sure which one to pick. Well, writing things down will help you get clarity. Some people feel scared thinking: "*OMG, if I write it down or think about it, it will become my reality.*" This is not the case, though!

You are just writing different options, and you intend to pick and choose the ones you like.

Also, remember, it's not about perfection, it's about progress. Getting clarity on what you want is hard for many people, and I have been there too. I remember when I first got introduced to the "design your ideal day exercise." It was actually during some business and marketing training, and I felt perplexed. I remember thinking, why don't they just show me how to grow a business and make more money? If they give me the best marketing strategy, then I will surely design a super great life.

What I didn't realize back then is that I was putting the cart before the horse. And well, when it comes to "marketing," manifestation is also like marketing. We market ourselves and our desires to the Universe. So, once again, we need clarity as to which desires we wish to market!

Remember when you were a kid? You had clarity. You knew what you wanted. You didn't hesitate when saying, "I guess this is not for me."

Well, you want to be that little kid, writing their wish list to Santa Claus (or whoever brings presents in your country/culture).

It's all a process, and your real vision will come. Start writing things down to get clarity. There's no way around it.

Question: Is there step-by-step guidance to help me write a detailed vision for all areas of my life?

Answer: Yes. To do it, focus on finance, health, personal relationships, professional relationships, lifestyle (your home, car, vacations), and physical appearance. Some people also like to add spiritual experiences, fulfillment, specific work, passions, etc.

Focus on what matters for you and your vision. For example, if you are an introvert and don't really like having a social life or attending big gatherings, there is no point in adding, "I go out and socialize every day" to your vision just for the sake of it. Unless, of course, you want to manifest becoming a social, extroverted person because it is your real goal.

It all goes back to what we covered in the introduction of this book; focus on goals that are genuinely yours. It's tempting to copy other people's visions, thinking, "*If they are doing well, they are successful, so I'm just gonna do the same.*"

This is a big no-no. Tune in with your heart. It knows! Unleash the Power of Self-Coaching, and you can be your primary source of information and inspiration.

Most people keep jumping to the past instead of jumping to their future. The best book you can ever read is your own journal because it is where you write your life, and this is what will get you results.

Below are some self-coaching questions to help you get even more clarity:

-What would you do if you knew you couldn't fail?

-How would that affect you and your recent decisions?

Question: I'm still a bit scared to get started. What if I do it the wrong way and don't manifest anything?

Answer: The only wrong way is when you overcomplicate it or do it as an obligation. You design your own rules! You are in control, and you are empowered to make decisions for yourself.

You are not in school anymore, and I'm not your teacher telling you to write an essay, in a specific style, with 3k words; no more, no less.

I am happy to be your guide and inspire you to get started to be self-sufficient and empowered. It's all about getting started, no matter what you do.

You seem to be stuck in a place of doubt (no judgment here; I have been there as well). Ask yourself: how would it feel to get unstuck by just getting started?

You have nothing to lose, but a lot to gain. This is what self-development is all about, and it should be fun.

You can also use the following steps:

Step #1 - Speak as though your wish had already come true.

Example: "*I am so happy and grateful now that...*

Step #2 - Start expressing your desires daily as though you are experiencing them in your now.

Example: "*I feel so grateful I feel so much energy every single day.*"

"*I'm getting more and more inspired, and my creativity is so abundant!*"

"*I feel so grateful that all of my relationships are positive and uplifting!*"

Step#3 - Look for love and positivity wherever you are. Always be thankful, and look for more and more things to be grateful for. Trust the Universe because it knows what's right for you and your long-term wellbeing.

Example: *"I'm so grateful to the Universe for allowing all of my dreams into my reality. I love the person I'm becoming. It feels so good."*

- *"I'm grateful that all these amazing opportunities align because the Universe cares for me."*

- *"I know that I'm not alone and that the Universe is always working to create more happiness for me."*

Step#4 - Show your commitment and dedication by taking inspired action in alignment with your vision. Use the following affirmations, or use them as a guide to creating your own that feel good for you:

- *"I'm so grateful for the opportunities I've been given, and I commit to being a vehicle of creativity."*

- *"I radiate my unique, authentic expression to the fullest of my capacity."*

- *"I express myself through my work, for the highest good of everyone involved."*

- *"I commit to being in alignment with my higher self. I share only good thoughts, actions, and feelings with those around me."*

- *"I commit to practicing powerful self-talk. I talk to myself kindly to unleash my full potential."*

Question: Do we have to re-write our script every day? Can we "copy" each day what we previously wrote?

Answer: First of all, get rid of "have to" and "should." Use the word "choose" instead. It's so much more empowering! So, yes, it's up to you. You can choose to re-write your vision if you want to, and you can also rephrase it or focus on some elements of it. It's up to you what you do. But the primary purpose behind it is to fuse yourself with your vision and use scripting methods as a tool.

Question: Can I script and write other things I experience in my life in my regular diary or journal at the same time? Will the Universe get confused on which is my actual scripting?

Answer: The Universe won't get confused unless you feel confused, so it's really up to you. If you want to have two different journals and it feels right for you, go for it. You can organize yourself in the way that best suits you.

Some people like to have just one journal, and they write their daily gratitude intertwined with their scripts. Some want to keep a diary to track what's going on in their head while using a different journal for scripting purposes.

The real question is: what feels right and sustainable for you?

Question:

I want to use scripting to manifest success faster. My dream is to be a businessman. I want to create a high income for myself and those who work for me. I want to build a big company. The problem is that I'm only 17. Do you think it's too early to start?

Answer: Don't ask other people or me for permission or approval. It's clear that you know what you want, and you used powerful, confident language. You also have your why, which is excellent. I think it's wonderful that you have such a big vision at such a young age and want to help other people by creating well-paying jobs for them.

However, you are also quick to negate your vision with a "but." Age is just a number, and you limit yourself by saying what you've said. Yes, legally, in most, if not all countries, you probably can't open a company at your age. But so what? You can still work on your vision and script. You can open your dream company in your mind.

At the same time, you can start taking aligned action by learning more about business. You can enjoy the journey and allow it to lead you to your destination. The mind and what you can achieve in life are limitless if you believe in yourself.

Question: Shall I script in my native language or in English?

Answer: Both are fine. While most people would feel more confident scripting in their mother tongue, there are some exceptions. For example, let's say your native language is French. However, you are also fluent in English, and you are used to reading and studying self-development books in English. In this case, your mind started learning these new concepts in your second language, which is English, and it makes some sense to stick to it in your scripting rituals. But, once again, do what feels right for you. You could even mix two languages if you want. The Universe will respond to your feelings and emotions, so feel free to write in whatever language you want.

Question: I usually write ten things I feel grateful for, and then I write my affirmations every day. Am I doing it right? Are "positive affirmations" and "scripting" the same things or different from each other?

Answer: If you feel good about what you do; use positive, empowering language; write your affirmations in the present tense, and are open to taking inspired action; there's no doubt something beautiful will come out of your endeavors. So, to answer your question, don't worry, you are doing it right. Now, when it comes to comparing scripting to affirmations, there is a little difference:

Affirmation is about writing positive statements.

For example, *Every day, I feel more and more energized.*

Scripting is writing your desires in a story format.

For example, *I wake up in my beautiful beach house. I can hear and smell the ocean. I get up, and I can see my beautiful blue carpet. I just got my Pedi done yesterday, and the nail polish matches my carpet. I go downstairs, drink water, and make myself a nice, nutritious smoothie. It's now 8 o'clock. My yoga teacher is coming at 9, so I'm going to have a quick shower now and then meditate a bit on my terrace. I feel so energized and healthy. It makes me feel excited about my day because I know that many amazing things are coming my way!*

The critical element here is to 'feel the emotions' while we write our desires. So, if you'd like to enhance your journaling practice, be sure to use more feelings in your writing. You can also write your vision in detail using dynamic scripting, then record it and listen to it every day. Pick whatever feels right for you.

Question: Can this be done on my phone instead of writing with pen and paper???

Answer: It could, as a plan B. However, I'd suggest the old-school option of using pen and paper. There's something magical about it, and it makes you feel like the designer and architect of your life.

Question: What do you think is the biggest reason for scripting not working out for someone?

Answer: Scripting will not work if a person is using it out of desperation, like a quick fix or technique, without fully understanding the essential principles of making your mind work for you, choosing goals that excite you, staying motivated while enjoying the journey, and doing the inner work while re-designing your self-image.

Question: I'm a bit insecure about having a journal because I'm afraid someone from my family could casually find it and read it? I would feel so stupid! I know I could record my vision, but then once again, what if someone discovers it? They would think I'm going mad!

Answer: If you're into any kind of self-development, some people will indeed think you're going mad, haha. So, first of all, you need to ask yourself, what do you care about more? Your vision, success, and happiness? Or what will other people think of you? Now imagine, as you manifest your desires, your current negative voices that say, *"what will other people think of me"* might amplify accordingly. So, first things first, I would address the resistance and possible inner insecurities you are experiencing. The technique I would recommend you use is called the Emotional Freedom Technique (EFT). One of the best books I've read on this topic is called *The Tapping Solution* by Nick Ortner. I always recommend it to my readers because I know it can help them take care of their emotional wellbeing and eliminate resistance.

While I'm not an expert on EFT or a certified practitioner, I've been using it on myself successfully for over three years now and have experienced some tremendous shifts with it.

Hopefully, my answer will help you address what I believe might be the more profound issue preventing you from smooth manifestations.

To answer your question more practically, you could purchase a diary or journal with a lock; or save your journals in a locked safe. You have the right to protect your space!

Question: I found the perfect journal for my scripting journey, but it has some writing in it on the first page. Can I rip it out? Will it affect my manifestations?

Answer: You worry too much. If you feel good about the first page, keep it as it is. Maybe it was meant to be there as some kind of a lesson from the Universe. However, if it feels off, you can get rid of it. Honestly, I don't see any reason why it could affect your goals and manifestations in life.

Question: I know what to do. I know I logically understand how it all works. But I can't truly feel my vision. I'm very clear on my desires, I know what kind of career I want, and how big my new salary is. I know everything. But, I can't see my new self. I can't experience the feelings my new self would feel. So, I write and script, but I know I do it automatically, like a robot. I can still stick to it because I'm very disciplined, but I know it won't be effective because I can't seem to feel anything. Is there anything I can do to connect with my new self-image and experience all those unique feelings to manifest my desires faster?

Answer: Well done on successfully spotting what you might be doing wrong. You are an excellent LOA detective! And don't worry too much, because reconnecting with your feelings for manifestation purposes might take some time, especially if you are a very logical person (from the way you write, I would say you are, but you are also open to feelings and spirituality, which will really help you on your manifestation journey).

To help you, I recommend that you start using one of my favorite Law of Attraction Meditations from the next chapter.

Chapter 6

Powerful Law of Attraction Meditation to Connect with Your Higher Self

This meditation is designed to help you raise your vibration. So that you can align with the best version of yourself and mindfully attract your desires.

Sit down in a comfortable position. Take a few deep breaths.

Start off with a big, big smile. It's your time. Your time to shine. Your time to grow and expand.

So that you can manifest more of what you truly desire.

Inhale. Take a deep breath and imagine an ample white light. It's the light of all the possibilities. Allow it. Breathe it in, and feel it in all the cells of your body. It's the light from the Universe that can make all your wishes come true.

Now, peacefully allow yourself to exhale all your doubts and fears. Let go of all past judgments, blame, guilt, and self-criticism.

Carry on breathing deeply and slowly. But don't force it. You can choose to speed up or slow down. It's really up to you. Whatever feels right for you at this moment.

Breathe in the light and exhale the dark.

Remember that you are raising your vibration as you do this, therefore automatically attracting more highly vibrational experiences, people, and things into your life.

Now, take a moment to look back at your journey and be grateful for how far you have come. You've been learning. You've been growing. You've been expanding. Just give yourself a few moments to reflect on how much you have grown in the last year, two years, and five years.

Allow yourself to be grateful for all the challenges you overcame.

You've grown so much, and you are getting stronger and stronger with every second, minute, and hour.

Now you know what you desire. You know how to attract it. You are patient. You are enjoying the journey. And you choose to focus on positivity. Take a moment to feel thoroughly proud of yourself and how far you've come.

Now, you can allow yourself to look ahead. You are releasing all the doubts and negativity from the past. Remember to keep breathing in positive white light while breathing out what's no longer serving you on your journey.

Now, see the New You. The more empowered you. You from the future. How do you feel?

How do you speak and act?

Are you calmer and more at peace? Are you more confident and empowered?

Allow these positive feelings to light up in every cell of your body. How does it feel to be that future version of you already?

Be aware that to manifest faster, our focus should be on our personal and spiritual growth. We attract what we are.

You attract who you become. So, who are you?

Allow yourself to feel that person in every cell of your body. Be that person; right here and right now.

The next level version of you is now sitting right before you. You are smiling at one another. Your future is looking at you with so much love, compassion, and understanding. It wants to teach you and guide you.

What is the message Your Future You wants to tell you today?

Give your higher self a big, big hug and allow it to hug you back. You now merge and become one. You become your higher self. You are your higher self now.

Now, activate your new self and let go of whatever old identity no longer serves you.

Letting go is easy; simply say *goodbye* and release all negativity from the past.

Clench your fists tight and feel your fingers in your palms. This tension represents your old self, your old habits, actions, and beliefs. Old ways that were preventing you from shining your light. Your old mindsets and all the judgment, criticism, and fear.

Feel the effort that is required to hold you in that old place.

Now, unclench your fists. Feel the resistance and become aware of how easy it can be if you just let it go.

Unclenching, relaxing, and living your life without tension, resistance, and old habits that no longer serve you feels so good.

Now, there is less effort and less tension, and your palms are open, so you are open to receiving more and more.

Open your fingers and allow every cell in your hands to start absorbing the new energy of abundance, love, and freedom. Feel that positive energy spread through your body.

Allow the energy to vibrate. Allow yourself to be empowered.

Wrap your arms around your shoulders and give yourself a hug. You are already ready to manifest your desires. You are already prepared to step into your dream life!

Give yourself a big hug.

Whisper: "*I am ready to receive*" to your heart.

Keep affirming: "*I am so proud of who I've become. I love the person I am now!*"

Take a deep inhale. Exhale and relax.

Also, remember you don't have to revert back to your old patterns. You have already merged with your new self. You are your unique self.

This is your real power. This is how amazing you are. Your higher self is right there with you. Your higher self is smiling at you now.

Whenever you feel worried or doubtful, visualize your higher self smiling at you and shining your light from within you.

Because it's you, it's who you indeed are!

Conclusion – Trust Yourself

Keep expanding and keep moving forward!

Remember that you attract who you are. So, keep aligning your thoughts, feelings, and actions with what you want. Watch your energy transform. Embody your desires. Be your desires. Affirm your desires with what you do and how you think about yourself, not only with what you say.

Don't get discouraged or impatient if it takes longer to manifest your desires; the journey itself is your destination. As you are exploring yourself and your manifestation abilities, you are becoming a better person. You are kind to yourself and others while cultivating a positive mindset infused with endless gratitude. That alone is a gift to those around you!

Keep practicing what you have learned, and keep sharing these concepts with others. Together we can change the world by collectively enhancing the vibration of the planet.

I genuinely hope that this book inspired you and gave you new tools to expand your consciousness and raise awareness.

You are limitless, you are powerful, and you are amazing!

I believe in you and wish you all the best on your journey!

If you have a few minutes, I'd really appreciate it if you could leave me a short review on Amazon. Let other LOA readers in our community know who this book can help, how, and why.

Thank You, Thank You, Thank You,
I hope we "meet" again,
Much love,

Elena

For more information and resources about LOA and manifestation, visit my website:

www.LOAforSuccess.com

If you'd like to say hi, please email me at: elena@LOAforSuccess.com

Join Our Manifestation Newsletter and Get a Free eBook

To help you AMPLIFY what you've learned in this book, I'd like to offer you a free copy of my LOA Workbook – a powerful, FREE 5-day program (eBook & audio) designed to help you raise your vibration while eliminating resistance and negativity.

To sign up for free, visit the link below now:
www.loaforsuccess.com/newsletter

You'll also get free access to my highly acclaimed, uplifting LOA Newsletter.

Through this email newsletter, I regularly share all you need to know about the manifestation mindset and energy.

My newsletter alone helped hundreds of my readers manifest their own desires.

Plus, whenever I release a new book, you can get it at a deeply discounted price or even for free.
 You can also start receiving my new audiobooks published on Audible at no cost!
To sign up for free, visit the link below now:
www.loaforsuccess.com/newsletter

I'd love to connect with you and stay in touch with you while helping you on your LOA journey!
If you happen to have any technical issues with your sign up, please email us at:

support@LOAforSuccess.com

More Books by Elena G. Rivers

Law of Attraction Short Reads Series

Money Mindset: Stop Manifesting What You Don't Want and Shift Your Subconscious Mind into Money & Abundance

How Not to Manifest: Manifestation Mistakes to Avoid and How to Finally Make LOA Work for You

Visualization Demystified: The Untold Secrets to Re-Program Your Subconscious Mind and Manifest Your Dream Reality in 5 Simple Steps

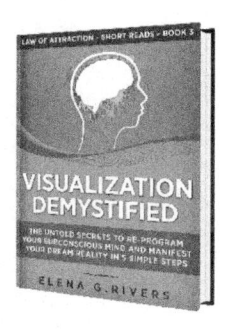

Law of Attr-Action for Entrepreneurs: Advanced Identity Shifting Secrets to Manifest the Income & Impact You Deserve

The Love of Attraction: Tested Secrets to Let Go of Fear-Based Mindsets, Activate LOA Faster, and Start Manifesting Your Desires!

Manifestation Secrets Demystified: Advanced Law of Attraction Techniques to Manifest Your Dream Reality by Changing Your Self-Image Forever

Printed in Great Britain
by Amazon